WE THE PEOPLE

The Boston Tea Party

by Michael Burgan

Content Adviser: Professor Sherry L. Field,
Department of Social Science Education, College of Education,
The University of Georgia

Reading Adviser: Dr. Linda D. Labbo,
Department of Reading Education, College of Education,
The University of Georgia

 COMPASS POINT BOOKS
Minneapolis, Minnesota

Compass Point Books
3722 West 50th Street, #115
Minneapolis, MN 55410

Visit Compass Point Books on the Internet at *www.compasspointbooks.com* or e-mail your request
to *custserv@compasspointbooks.com*

Photographs ©: North Wind Picture Archives, cover, 6; Archive Photos, 7; North Wind Picture
Archives, 8, 10; FPG International, 11; North Wind Picture Archives, 12, 13, 15, 16; Archive
Photos, 18; North Wind Picture Archives, 20, 21, 22; Archive Photos, 24; North Wind Picture
Archives, 27, 28; FPG International, 31; Photri-Microstock, 32; North Wind Picture Archives, 34;
FPG International/Jack Zehrt, 37; North Wind Picture Archives, 38; FPG International, 40.

Editors: E. Russell Primm and Emily J. Dolbear
Photo Researcher: Svetlana Zhurkina
Photo Selector: Dawn Friedman
Design: Bradfordesign, Inc.
Cartography: XNR Productions, Inc.

Library of Congress Cataloging-in-Publication Data

Burgan, Michael.
   The Boston Tea Party / by Michael Burgan.
    p. cm. — (We the people)
Includes bibliographical references and index.
   Summary: Recounts the events leading up to the colonists' defiant act against the British known
as the Boston Tea Party, which ultimately climaxed in the American Revolution.
   ISBN 0-7565-0040-0
    1. Boston Tea Party, 1773—Juvenile literature. [1. Boston Tea Party, 1773. 2. United States—
History—Revolution, 1775–1783—Causes.] I. Title. II. We the people (Compass Point Books)
   E215.7 .B87 2000
   973.3'115—dc21
                                                                           00-008669

TABLE OF CONTENTS

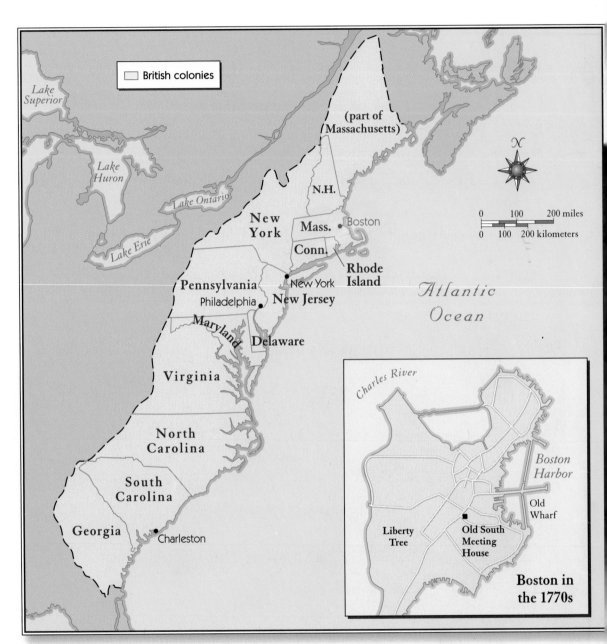

The thirteen colonies and Bosto

AN IMPORTANT TOWN MEETING

It was December 16, 1773. In Boston Harbor, three wooden ships quietly bobbed in the water. The moon cast almost no light that cold night. British sailors on the ships guarded a special cargo—342 chests of tea.

Just a few blocks away from the ships in the harbor, more than 7,000 citizens were gathered at the Old South Meeting House. It was the largest crowd ever seen at a single town meeting in Boston, Massachusetts.

The people were discussing the British ships. Many did not want the cargo to be unloaded from the ships. They wanted the three ships to return to

England with their tea. Thomas Hutchinson, the governor of Massachusetts, disagreed. The ships would leave Boston only after the tea was unloaded.

Samuel Adams rose to speak. He was a leader of the **Patriots**. The Patriots were American colonists who were angry about Britain's tax on tea. They felt the British government had no right to collect taxes, since

Thomas Hutchinson

6

Americans had no representatives in the British government. "Taxation without representation is **tyranny**" was their popular cry.

Finally, Adams said, "This meeting can do nothing more to save the country!" The Boston Tea Party was about to begin.

Samuel Adams

7

British troops in the French and Indian War

8

THE ROAD TO THE TEA PARTY

For ten years, Britain had tried to collect taxes from the Americans. In 1763, Britain had defeated France in the French and Indian War. This war was fought mainly in North America. It had been a costly war for King George III of Britain. The king and his government, called **Parliament**, were short of money. They decided to tax the thirteen American **colonies**. The money from the taxes would help pay to defend North America.

The Sugar Act of 1764 called for a tax on everything made from sugar. The next year, Parliament passed the Stamp Act. This law called for a tax on all printed things—even playing cards!

British tax stamps

The Stamp Act made many Americans angry. The Americans were not used to paying taxes to Britain. They had ruled themselves for years. Crowds of colonists attacked the people who tried to collect the new taxes. These tax collectors were sometimes tarred and feathered—covered with hot tar and bird feathers from pillows.

Colonists tar and feather a tax collector.

Samuel Adams led the opposition to the Stamp Act in Boston. He helped form the Sons of Liberty. They were a group of Patriots who wanted to take action against England. Other

A meeting of Patriots

Colonists protesting the Stamp Act in New York

colonies soon had their own Sons of Liberty
groups. Their loud protests finally convinced
Britain to get rid of the Stamp Act.

But Parliament still thought it had the right to tax the colonists. In 1767, it set up many new taxes. Bostonians again took to the streets in protest. In response, England put armed troops in the city. During the next few years, people across the colonies complained about the taxes.

The presence of the English soldiers in Boston sparked more anger. Tensions between Boston citizens and the English soldiers, or **redcoats**, led to the **Boston Massacre**. Five people were killed after a mob threw stones at a group of redcoats.

On March 5, 1770, the same day as the Boston Massacre, Parliament decided to remove most of its taxes. Only the tea tax remained. The tax was three **pence** on 1 pound (0.4 kilogram) of tea.

English soldiers fire on colonists in the Boston Massacre.

Wealthy ladies and gentlemen having tea

TEATIME IN THE COLONIES

For most Americans, a tax on tea was especially insulting. Tea had become a popular drink in the colonies. By some counts, American used more than 2 million pounds (908,000 kg) of tea every year. Most Boston residents drank at least two cups a day.

The Patriots started an anti-tea movement. They asked colonists to drink local herbs instead of tea from Britain. Some tea drinkers also turned to tea that had been **smuggled**—carried illegally into America without being taxed. Bostonians found it hard to be without their beloved tea. One Patriot said, "they would part with all their liberties, and religion too, rather than renounce [tea]."

NOTHING WAS THOUGHT OF BUT THIS TAXATION,
AND THE EASIEST METHOD OF LIQUIDATION.

T-A-X

'TWAS ENOUGH TO VEX
THE SOULS OF THE MEN OF BOSTON TOWN,
TO READ THIS UNDER THE SEAL OF THE CROWN.

TAX·ON
TEA·
3ᵈ per lb

1773

THEY WERE LOYAL SUBJECTS OF GEORGE THE THIRD;
SO THEY BELIEVED AND SO THEY AVERRED,
BUT THIS BRISTLING, OFFENSIVE PLACARD SET
ON THE WALLS, WAS WORSE THAN A BAYONET,

A notice announcing the tax on tea

The anti-tea movement had one major effect. The company that controlled the British tea trade, the East India Company, began to lose money. In an effort to help the company, Parliament passed the Tea Act in 1773. This law said that only the East India Company could sell tea to the American colonies. The East India Company then hired people to sell the tea and collect the tax. These tax collectors were called agents.

The Patriots once again reacted strongly. They were upset about the choice of agents. In Boston, these agents included the governor's brother and son. Governor Hutchinson had opposed the Patriots in Boston since 1765. Now, the tea crisis set him and his family against the Patriots.

THE TEA COMES TO AMERICA

In September 1773, seven ships left London, England. Between them, the ships carried almost 2,000 wooden chests. Each chest was filled with about 360 pounds (163 kg) of East India Company tea.

The ships sailed for Boston; New York City; Philadelphia, Pennsylvania; and Charleston, South Carolina. Within a few weeks, the colonists knew that the tea was on its way across the ocean.

The coat of arms of the East India Company

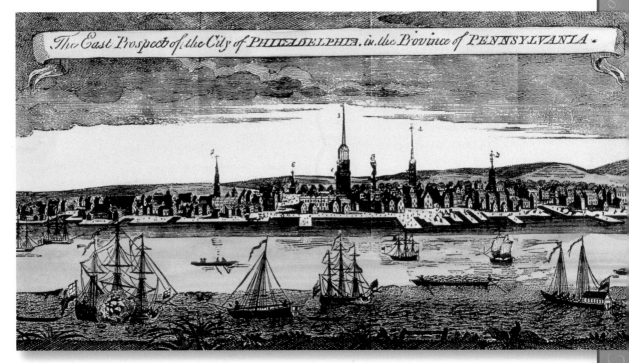

The port of Philadelphia

In New York and Philadelphia, the Patriots started trying to turn back the tea ships almost as soon as they knew they were coming. They wrote threatening letters to the tea agents in their cities. They warned local harbor guides not to help bring the ships to port. And the Patriots talked again about taxation without representation. If the

21

colonists took the tea and paid the tax, what other taxes would follow?

The anti-tea campaign worked. Tea agents in New York and Philadelphia quit their jobs before the tea arrived. The ships headed for those ports returned to Britain. Tea was unloaded in Charleston, but it was stored in a warehouse and never sold. Meanwhile, the Patriots were planning their strategy for rejecting the tea.

Ships in Charleston harbor

BOSTON'S FIRST SHIP ARRIVES

Samuel Adams and the Sons of Liberty led the attack against Boston's tea agents. At each agent's home, they left a message about a big public meeting. On November 3, 1773, about 1,000 people gathered at the meeting place—a huge elm tree known as the Liberty Tree. Patriots often met there to discuss public events and protest against British laws. But when the meeting began, the tea agents were not there.

For the next few weeks, Adams and his supporters tried to get the agents to give up their jobs. They also asked Governor Hutchinson to turn back the tea ships when they arrived. But the governor was loyal to Britain and always refused.

TO THE
DELAWARE
PILOTS.

THE Regard we have for your Characters, and our Desire to promote your future Peace and Safety, are the Occasion of this Third Address to you.

    In our second Letter we acquainted you, that the Tea Ship was a Three Decker; We are now informed by good Authority, she is not a Three Decker, but an *old black Ship, without a Head,* or *any Ornaments.*

    THE *Captain* is a *short fat* Fellow, and a little *obstinate* withal.----So much the worse for him.----For, so sure as he *rides rusty,* We shall heave him Keel out, and see that his Bottom be well fired, scrubb'd and paid.----His Upper-Works too, will have an Overhawling----and as it is said, he has a good deal of *Quick Work* about him, We will take particular Care that such Part of him undergoes a thorough Rummaging.

    WE have a still *worse* Account of *his* Owner ;----for it is said, the Ship POLLY was bought by him on Purpose, to make a Penny of us ; and that *he* and Captain *Ayres* were well advised of the Risque they would run, in thus daring to insult and abuse us.

    Captain Ayres was here in the Time of the Stamp-Act, and ought to have known our People better, than to have expected we would be so mean as to suffer his *rotten* TEA to be funnel'd down our Throats, with the *Parliament's Duty* mixed with it.

    WE know him well, and have calculated to a Gill and a Feather, how much it will require to fit him for an *American Exhibition.* And we hope, not one of your Body will behave so ill, as to oblige us to clap him in the Cart along Side of the *Captain.*

    WE must repeat, that the SHIP POLLY is an *old black Ship,* of about Two Hundred and Fifty Tons burthen, *without a Head,* and *without Ornaments,*----and, that CAPTAIN AYRES is a *thick chunky Fellow.*----------As such, TAKE CARE to AVOID THEM.

YOUR OLD FRIENDS,

THE COMMITTEE FOR TARRING AND FEATHERING.

Philadelphia, December 7, 1773.

This notice threatened a ship's crew with tarring and feathering if it unloaded tea.

24

By this time, Governor Hutchinson had a strong personal hatred for Adams too, and the Patriot leader returned the feeling.

On November 28, 1773, word spread quickly through Boston: the first tea ship had arrived. The *Dartmouth* was anchored in Boston Harbor. It held 114 chests of tea. Once the tea reached land, the colonists would have to pay the tax on it.

The Patriots had to find a way to keep the tea from coming ashore. They also knew they had a deadline for this task—midnight, December 16, 1773.

The Patriots went into action. They called a meeting for November 29, 1773. Messages were sent to committees of political leaders in nearby towns. These committees sent messages to each other during times of trouble. Adams had set up the first committee in 1772. Now the Boston Patriots wanted as much support as possible.

British troops were still in Boston. They were stationed at Castle William, an island fort in the harbor. And British warships under the command of Admiral John Montagu were in the harbor.

A rumor spread that soldiers might try to unload the ship. Armed patriots guarded the *Dartmouth* to make sure no one tried to remove the tea. Many citizens of Boston bought pistols in case things turned violent. Fearing for their safety, the tea agents had already fled to Castle William.

Although Governor Hutchinson was in charge, he spent most of his time outside Boston. As the crisis went on, the Boston committee began to act as the local government. The committee tried to persuade Francis Rotch, the owner of

The fort at Castle William

The tea party plot was planned in this building.

the *Dartmouth*, to sail his ship out of Boston Harbor. Rotch wouldn't agree unless Hutchinson supported it. Meanwhile, the governor ordered Admiral Montagu to stop any ship that tried to leave the harbor.

By December 13, 1773, a second tea ship, the *Eleanor*, had arrived in Boston. The *Eleanor* and the *Dartmouth* were tied up at Griffin's Wharf, where a third ship, the *Beaver*, soon joined them. That day, the Boston committee met with the committees from other towns.

The meeting, held in secret, lasted late into the night. At this meeting, the Patriots probably made their final plans for ending the tea crisis. The December 16 deadline was quickly approaching.

Throwing a Tea Party

The huge town meeting of December 16 started in the morning. Samuel Adams and others spoke to the crowd. Their speeches passed the time while everyone waited to hear if Hutchinson had changed his mind about releasing the ships.

Francis Rotch had been sent to Hutchinson, and around 6 P.M., he returned with the governor's reply. The owner of the *Dartmouth* explained that he could not take his ship out of the harbor. Just then, someone in the crowd shouted, "Who knows how well tea mingles with seawater?" The people cheered.

A few moments later, Adams gave the signal for action. Suddenly, loud war whoops filled the meeting hall. A group of Patriots stood at the

The great tea meeting

doorway. They had covered their skin with soot or
paint and wrapped blankets around their heads.
This costume was supposed to make the Patriots
look like Native Americans. At least the disguise
would hide their identity during the risky raid

Patriots dressed as Indians board the English tea ships.

they were about to make. This raid became known
as the Boston Tea Party.

The "Indians" led a mob through the streets
of Boston to Griffin's Wharf. The Patriots used
axes to hack through the tea chests. They also

32

carried guns to defend themselves in case the British troops attacked. The soldiers at Castle William heard about the Tea Party, but they did not come to the harbor.

Admiral Montagu, in Boston that night, also knew of the raid. He wrote the next day, "I could easily have prevented the execution of this plan but must have endangered the lives of many innocent people by firing upon the town." The British did not want another Boston Massacre, so the Tea Party went on.

The Patriots formed three groups, one for each ship in the harbor. The men worked silently and tried not to hurt the sailors on board or damage the ships. They simply wanted to destroy all the tea. The only injury came when a Patriot was hit on the head by a piece of equipment used

33

Destroying chests of tea

to lift the heavy chests of tea. He was knocked out but recovered quickly.

The entire raid took just under three hours. The tide was low at the time, so piles of tea formed next to the ships. Some of the "Indians" had to go into the water and scatter the tea. When it was over, the Patriots removed their shoes and poured out any tea that had fallen in. This tea also drifted into the cold waters of Boston Harbor.

No one knows for sure who carried out this daring raid. Historians think Paul Revere was one of the "Indians." Years after the Tea Party, many people claimed to have been there. Most of the raiders were young men, perhaps as young as fourteen. Whoever took part, they played an important role in creating an independent America.

AFTER THE TEA PARTY

When he heard about the Tea Party, Governor Hutchinson was shocked and angry. He called the raid an "outrage." He labeled the Patriots "lawless and highly criminal."

Hutchinson hoped the men responsible would be arrested. But the governor knew most people in Boston would turn against anyone who identified the Patriots. No one was ever arrested for the raid.

In the days after the Boston Tea Party, the Patriots and their supporters celebrated. One of the city's newspapers, the *Boston Gazette,* reported that the citizens "are almost universally congratulating each other on this happy event."

Patriot songs praised the Tea Party:

"A NOBLE SIGHT—to see the accursed TEA

Mingled with MUD—and ever for to be;

For KING and PRINCE shall know that we

are FREE."

John Adams, a cousin
of Samuel Adams and
another leading
Patriot, felt the raid
would be considered
a historic event.
Adams was right.

John Adams

Carpenter's Hall in Philadelphia, the site of the First Continental Congress

FINAL STEPS TO THE REVOLUTION

Almost immediately, the British responded to the Boston Tea Party. They sent more soldiers to Boston and closed the city's port. Parliament also placed the entire state of Massachusetts under a military governor and limited the power of local governments.

The Americans called these actions the Intolerable Acts. They angered the people and brought the colonies together. In every colony, many people were ready to oppose these new laws. The restrictions that the British now placed on the citizens of Massachusetts could someday be placed on them too.

The Battle of Lexington

In September 1774, delegates from all the colonies except Georgia met in Philadelphia, Pennsylvania. They formed the First Continental Congress.

The representatives discussed how the colonies should respond to the Intolerable Acts. The Congress decided that the colonies would not accept any goods from Britain. They also promised to support Massachusetts if the British used force against it.

Tensions on both sides continued to build. On April 19, 1775, Patriots and British soldiers met at Lexington and Concord in Massachusetts, firing "the shot heard 'round the world." The American Revolution had begun. And the Boston Tea Party had set in motion the events that led to that war.

GLOSSARY

Boston Massacre—a street riot in Boston in which five people were killed

colonies—the thirteen British territories that became the United States of America

Parliament—the British government

Patriots—American colonists who wanted independence from England

pence—British pennies

redcoats—British soldiers in America, named for the color of their uniforms

smuggled—carried illegally

tyranny—unfair or brutal power

DID YOU KNOW?

- Tea was introduced in England in 1657. England was then the only European country where people preferred tea to coffee.

- The tea on the British ships attacked during the Boston Tea Party was grown in China.

- After the Boston Tea Party, Governor Thomas Hutchinson returned to England to advise King George III.

- Since the American Revolution, tea has never competed successfully with coffee as the main hot drink in North America.

IMPORTANT DATES

Timeline

1763	England defeats France in the French and Indian War.
1764	Parliament passes the Sugar Act, a tax on foods made of sugar.
1765	Parliament passes the Stamp Act, a tax on all printed items.
1770	Five colonists are killed during the Boston Massacre on March 5.
1773	Parliament passes the Tea Act, a tax on tea; the Boston Tea Party takes place on December 16.

IMPORTANT PEOPLE

SAMUEL ADAMS
(1722–1803), *leader of the Patriots*

GEORGE III
(1738–1820), *king of England from 1760 to 1820*

THOMAS HUTCHINSON
(1711–1780), *governor of the Massachusetts colony*

WANT TO KNOW MORE?

At the Library

Kroll, Steven. *The Boston Tea Party*. New York: Holiday House, 1998.

Monke, Ingrid. *Boston*. Minneapolis, Minn.: Dillon Press, 1988.

O'Neill, Laurie A. *The Boston Tea Party*. Brookfield, Conn.:
  Millbrook Press, 1996.

Stein, R. Conrad. *The Boston Tea Party*. Danbury, Conn.:
  Children's Press, 1996.

On the Web

From Revolution to Reconstruction

http://odur.let.rug.nl/~usa.htm

A wide range of information about American history from the colonial
period to modern times

The History Place: American Revolution

http://www.historyplace.com/unitedstates/revolution/index.html

A complete chronology of the Revolutionary War

Liberty! The American Revolution

http://www.pbs.org/ktca/liberty/

An online companion to the PBS series about the American Revolution

Through the Mail

Great Boston Convention and Tourism Bureau

Two Copley Place, Suite 105

Boston, MA 02116-6501

To get more information about visiting Boston

On the Road

Boston Tea Party Ship and Museum

Congress Street Bridge

Boston, MA 02110

617/338-1773

http://historictours.com

To visit the *Beaver II*, a reconstruction of one of the three tea ships

INDEX

About the Author

Michael Burgan is a freelance writer for both children and adults.
A history graduate of the University of Connecticut, he has written
more than thirty fiction and nonfiction children's books for various
publishers. For adult audiences, he has written news articles, essays,
and plays. Michael Burgan is a recipient of an Edpress Award and
belongs to the Society of Children's Book Writers and Illustrators.